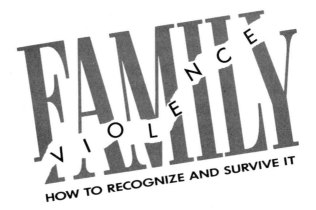

**FAMILY VIOLENCE**

HOW TO RECOGNIZE AND SURVIVE IT

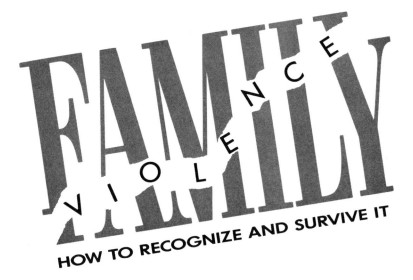

# FAMILY VIOLENCE

## HOW TO RECOGNIZE AND SURVIVE IT

Janice E. Rench

Lerner Publications Company • Minneapolis

LIBRARY OF CONGRESS CATALOGING-IN-PUBLICATION DATA

Rench, Janice E.
  Family violence : how to recognize and survive it / Janice E. Rench.
       p.   cm.
  Includes bibliographical references and index.
  Summary: Discusses various forms of family violence, including child abuse, sibling abuse, incest, and elder abuse, and discusses how to get help as well as ways of building self-esteem.
  ISBN 0-8225-0047-7
  1. Family violence—United States—Juvenile literature. 2. Self-respect in children—Juvenile literature. [1. Family violence. 2. Self-respect.] I. Title.
HQ809.3.U5R46   1992
362.82'92—dc20                                    91-21099
                                                       CIP
                                                       AC

Manufactured in the United States of America

1  2  3  4  5  6  7  8  9  10  01  00  99  98  97  96  95  94  93  92

## Acknowledgments

To Sonia Ferencik, Child Advocate Director, Templum House, Cleveland, Ohio, my deepest respect and thanks for her commitment to children, which was reflected in the extra time she took to review the manuscript so that the children's voices were heard.

To Anne Tapp, Co-Chair, Child Advocacy Task Force of the National Coalition Against Domestic Violence, Washington, D.C., my appreciation for the support she gave to this book.

To my editor, LeeAnne Engfer, who continues to teach with patience and understanding, my sincere appreciation.

To Larry, who suffers with me through each word, thanks for your support.

*Dedicated to the people
who have lived the pages of this book,
for their courage and hope,
which sustained them through their suffering.*

# CONTENTS

# FOREWORD

Most adults believe that home is a place to keep young people safe and protected from the scariness of the world. For some young people, home is this safe, protected place. But for many others, it is not. For those children and young people who live in violent families, home is not a shelter from the scariness of the world; rather, home is where that scariness begins.

Each year, hundreds of thousands of children and young people are abused by being hit, kicked, screamed at, called names, fondled, raped, degraded, hurt, and humiliated by the people who are supposed to love and care for them most—their families. Each year, millions of children and young people watch as one parent (most often Dad) batters and abuses the other parent (most often Mom). This is the world into which many children are born. This is the harsh reality.

If you live in a home where physical, sexual, or emotional abuse against yourself or another family member occurs, then this book is for you. If you live in a family that is violence-free, then this book is for you, too. In this book you will find stories that may help you to understand your own experiences or the experiences of a friend. You will also find information that can help you know that you are not alone, that family violence is not your fault, and that there are people and organizations that can assist you and your family.

The United States is one of the most violent societies in the world. Whether we like it or not, or intend to or not, our society teaches children that it is okay to use violence to get what you want. We make violence look cool and sexy. The tougher you are, the more people will respect you. Even entertainment created for young people is violent. (Can you imagine a nonviolent version of the Teenage Mutant Ninja Turtles?)

It is almost impossible to grow up in the United States without having personally experienced violence—through family violence, neighborhood or gang violence, or violent school discipline. Because violence is so accepted, it becomes very easy to use violence yourself as a way to solve problems, or to believe that it is all right for others (especially adults) to use physical, sexual, or emotional violence against you. Nothing could be further from the truth.

All young people deserve to have safe, healthy surroundings; to be given the chance to learn and grow and be happy; and to be respected and valued for who they are. You have the right to be treated with respect and honor simply because you are you.

As a society, we must begin spending more time, energy, and money to make sure that young people receive the respect and care they deserve. This means taking a very serious look at the way our society allows and encourages the use of violence. An important place to start is to begin talking about—and doing something about—child abuse and domestic violence.

At the National Coalition Against Domestic Violence, we believe that all of us have a part to play in creating a nonviolent society. For some, this means opposing people and groups who use violence to control others. For others, this means working to create laws that protect the victims and survivors of family violence. For still others, this means providing support and care for those whose homes have become a war zone.

What will your part be? After reading this book, you may want to ask yourself what you can do to make the world a safer, gentler place for yourself and others.

Anne M. Tapp, M.T.S.
The National Coalition Against Domestic Violence
Co-Chair, Child Advocacy Task Force

# INTRODUCTION

A family is more than just a group of people who live together. We learn about, and receive, love and affection in our families. Families come in all sizes, shapes, and colors. Maybe your family is you and your mother; you and your grandparents; you and your brothers and sisters; your father and his girlfriend; or your mother and your stepfather. You might live with an aunt and uncle and their children, with a gay or lesbian parent and his or her partner, with a foster family, or with an adopted family. Maybe you live with both your father and mother.

Regardless of whom you live with, your family is important to you. You look to the adults in your family to take care of you and provide the things you will need to become an independent adult. Our basic needs are food, shelter, and clothing. But children and young adults also need love, attention, comfort, and encouragement.

Most adults want the best for their children and work hard to provide that. Unfortunately, not all adults know what is best for young people. They may not know because no one gave them the things they needed when they were children. Maybe they were emotionally, physically, verbally, or sexually abused as children and believe that abuse is a natural part of family life. Whatever the reason, instead of giving love and affection, family members sometimes abuse and even seriously injure one another. This is called family violence.

Family violence or abuse is the mistreatment of one family member by another. Family violence can include many different kinds of abuse:

- *physical abuse*—slapping, punching, burning, hitting, pushing, biting
- *verbal abuse*—hurtful statements like "You're stupid," "You're ugly," "I wish you were never born," and "I hate you," or threats like "If you do that again, I will kill you (send you away) (get out the strap)"
- *emotional abuse*—being denied love or affection; neglect (not being given proper clothing, attention, food, or housing)
- *sexual abuse*—being touched in a way that is sexual or unwelcome, being forced to touch someone else, being forced to have intercourse, being made to look at sexual photographs or movies
- *domestic violence*—witnessing the adults who live with you hitting or abusing each other or another family member

Violence against children has a long history. The phrase in the Bible, "Spare the rod and spoil the child," was used to justify physical punishment of children. In colonial America, infanticide (the killing of infants) was legal, as was hitting children with rods, whips, and canes.

In 1874, church workers in New York City found out that a girl named Mary Ellen was being physically abused by her foster parents. The workers recognized that she needed help, but they didn't know where to turn. Finally, they called the Society for the Prevention of Cruelty to Animals, arguing that the girl was part of the animal kingdom. After this incident, the Society for the Prevention of Cruelty to Children was established. It wasn't until the end of the 1960s, however, that all states had passed laws requiring child abuse and neglect to be reported to the police.

In the past, laws supported the right of a husband to use force against his wife. The saying "rule of thumb" comes from a law that allowed a husband to beat his wife with a switch (a whip) as long as it was no wider than his thumb.

In the early 1970s, violence against women began to receive public attention. At the beginning of the women's movement, women gathered in small groups to discuss the issues that affected them. They discovered that many of them shared similar experiences of family violence. At the same time, the first public shelter for abused wives was established. In 1976, women's groups in the U.S. began a political movement to change laws and expand rights for women.

Family violence occurs among people of all ages, races, and religions. It happens to people of all educational and income levels. It is very common. This book is about family violence. At the end of each chapter is a list of questions you can answer to see if your family is violent. You will also find ideas about how to get help.

# CHAPTER ONE

# *Physical Abuse*

"Get up! Get up now or so help me God, I will kill you!"

The words hung in the air for a second, then seemed to vibrate off the walls and through the house.

Elizabeth felt her stomach tighten as she watched from the corner of her room, across from the kitchen. She could see her father standing over her older sister, Jean, who was hunched down on her knees near the kitchen sink. Afraid to move away, Elizabeth covered her face with her doll. She was afraid her father would notice her and come after her, too. Peeking out from around her doll, she saw her father pull Jean up by the hair and force her to her feet.

"You liar! When are you going to stop your lying? You were born stupid and you'll die stupid," he yelled, shaking Jean by the hair.

Jean's face became tight and red. To Elizabeth, Jean looked like a rag doll being shaken.

Elizabeth put her hands over her ears so she wouldn't hear the awful words her father was saying or the sound of him slapping her sister's face. She wondered why Jean always got such awful beatings. Elizabeth wished she could stop her father. But she knew she had to stay out of his way when he was in one of his "moods." She wondered how Jean could stand the pain. She always had bruises, but no one seemed to notice. Elizabeth never knew what to do, so she just sat very still, scared, knowing the screaming and hitting would eventually stop. Until the next time.

**What is child abuse?**

Child abuse is physical or mental injury done to a child by the person or persons who are responsible for the child's care and well-being.

**Why do parents physically abuse their children?**

Sometimes parents deal with their anger or stress by taking it out on their children. Adults who were physically abused themselves when they were young may do the same thing to their own children. Many parents start to abuse their children as a way to discipline them or teach good behavior.

**What is the difference between discipline and abuse?**

Most parents want the best for their children. Adults have the right to raise their children as they choose, including disciplining them. Parents also have the right to expect proper behavior from their children. Each family has different rules, values, and expectations, which are usually determined by cultural standards, religious views, and how the parents were brought up.

In a family with reasonable rules, you grow up feeling secure and loved. For example, maybe you were not allowed to watch your favorite television program if you didn't clean your room. Your parents taught you that if you got your chores done first, then you earned the right to relax and do fun things. Discipline is meant to teach acceptable behavior by helping you make good choices.

Physical abuse, on the other hand, causes pain. Physical punishment is used to control behavior, but it can lead to injury. When parents use physical punishment as a way to discipline their child, they teach that the way to deal with feelings and problems is through hitting.

### Why can't adults control their behavior?

Most adults who abuse others have trouble handling their feelings of anger. They find it difficult to resolve conflicts and problems in healthy, nonviolent ways. Adults may feel pressure from a job or from not having a job, or from unpaid bills, poor relationships, loneliness, health problems, or the feeling of being trapped. Maybe they don't have other adults to turn to for emotional support when these pressures become too much to handle. Whatever the adult's problem, however, there is never an excuse for violence, and it is never okay to hurt someone else physically.

### Are people abusive because they use alcohol or drugs?

You may live in a home where people use alcohol and drugs. Using drugs lowers one's ability to deal with problems in a healthy way. It can hurt someone's ability to maintain self-control. Drugs or alcohol may contribute to family violence, but their use does not excuse violent behavior.

### How was Elizabeth affected by seeing her sister hit?

No matter how old you are, it can be very frightening to see or hear the people you love and depend on abusing someone else or being abused. If you live in a violent home, you learn that violence is a powerful way to gain control over others. Elizabeth felt scared, alone, confused, and sad when she saw her sister get hurt.

### Why didn't someone notice Jean's bruises?

Often, people outside the family don't know that abuse is happening. You may be told not to discuss "family business" with outsiders. You might hear threats like, "You're my kid and I'll do what I want with you. It's no one else's business." Child abuse, however, is not just a "family matter"—it is against the law. Since physical abuse can result in death, it is very important that you report the abuse. If you, your brothers, or sisters are being hurt, tell an adult.

### Who could Jean turn to?

Jean (or Elizabeth) could tell a teacher, her religious leader, a school counselor, her best friend's mother or father, an aunt or uncle, or any adult whom she trusts. She could also call the police, a kids' telephone hotline, or a runaway shelter hotline. If the first person she tells can't or won't help her, then she must tell someone else and keep telling until someone helps stop the abuse.

### What happens when abuse is reported?

When the police or a social service agency receive a report of child abuse, an officer or an agency worker looks into the matter. He or she will ask you questions, such as the name of the person being abused, that person's address and telephone number, the parent's name, your relationship to the abused person, and, possibly, whether you witnessed the abuse. If you are reporting your own abuse, you need to tell everything that happened. The worker will investigate the situation by interviewing the person you say is abusing you. In many towns and cities, a child protection service can make decisions about the family. If the agency finds that a family member is at risk of being injured, it might remove the victim or the abuser from the home.

### How can I get help if I feel unsafe?

Find the phone number for Child Protection Services in your community and call them. If there isn't a number listed in your phone book, look under "Family Services" or call any crisis hotline. Many larger cities have shelters that you can call or go to for help. If you are afraid you will be in danger if your abusive parent finds out that you told someone, make sure to let the person you're telling know that. *Do not run away from home without having a safe place to go.* As painful as the abuse is at home, life on the streets is even worse.

### Signs of Physical Abuse

- Do you have any injuries caused by severe beatings?
- Have you been hit with a belt, board, electrical cord, or heavy object?
- Have you been burned intentionally by cigarettes, matches, scalding water, electrical appliances, or the stove?
- Have you been held under water, tied up to a chair or bed, or locked in the cellar, attic, or closet?

- Have your arms or fingers been bent backwards?
- Have you been locked out of the house or left alone all night?
- Have you been shaken violently until you couldn't see straight?
- Have you been lifted by your hair?

*If one or more of these things have happened or are happening to you or someone you know, tell someone who can help you.* You have the right to be free from violence and abuse.

# CHAPTER TWO

# *Emotional Abuse*

"Where's Mama?" Nina asked her younger sister, who was playing on an old rubber tire next to the garage.

"I don't know."

"Is she up yet?"

"Nah."

Nina leaned against the garage and watched her five-year-old sister as she spit on the dirty tire and rubbed the saliva around with her finger. The only clean spot on Natalie's face was a white streak running down from her nostril to her upper lip. The one button holding her jacket closed looked as if it were ready to pop off. The jacket sleeves stopped above her small, bony wrists. Although it was three o'clock in the afternoon, Nina had a feeling her sister hadn't eaten all day.

"Did Mama make you something to eat?"

"Nah."

"Who got you dressed this morning?

"Me."

"Great job," Nina said. Looking Natalie up and down, her eyes stopped at her feet. "You forgot your socks," Nina said as she walked away.

Nina walked up the back stairs to the kitchen. As she opened the door she could smell garbage. Dirty dishes were still piled on the table from last night's supper. She went into the dining room and added her schoolbooks to the pile of papers, half-empty coffee cups, clothes, and old newspapers on the table. Nina didn't see her mother in the living room—she was probably still in bed upstairs.

Nina hated coming home. She never knew where her mother would be or what kind of mood she would be in. Nina felt much older than twelve; she worried constantly about her mother and younger sister. She worried that her mother would leave and never come back. When her mother slept all day, Nina never knew if she should wake her up or leave her alone. Sometimes her mother screamed at her for waking her up, but other times she got mad if she let her sleep too long.

Not knowing what to do or what to expect from one day to the next made Nina tense and sick to her stomach. She had trouble sleeping at night, and it was hard to concentrate at school. She wished she could play with her friends after school, but she always had to come right home.

The worst part for Nina was not knowing if her mother cared about her or not. She didn't think she did. Especially since last week when she told her mother that her birthday was coming and her mother said angrily, "Don't remind me of when you were born."

Nina walked back through the kitchen. Although she was supposed to be working on a school project, she went to the back door and called her little sister in. The project would have to wait. No one cared how she was doing in school anyway, she thought, as she dampened a washcloth for Natalie's face.

### What is emotional abuse?

Emotional abuse happens when one or both of your parents frequently yells at you, calls you ugly names, or just ignores you. Emotional abuse affects your self-esteem and confidence. Here are some forms of emotional abuse:

- Being left alone for long periods of time
- Being threatened with monsters, bogeymen, or the police if you don't do something you're told
- Being forbidden to play with cousins, neighbors, or friends, or not being allowed to attend school
- Being called names like "dummy" or "stupid," or being told by an adult that he or she wishes you hadn't been born
- Being blamed for problems in the family
- Being forced to sell drugs or alcohol, to steal, or to do other illegal activities
- Being denied proper food, clothing, or medical care

### Is Nina being emotionally abused?

Yes, both Nina and her little sister are being emotionally abused. Nina has been forced to take over many adult jobs, such as taking care of the house, looking after her sister, and worrying about her mother, when she should be enjoying her own childhood.

### How does it feel to be emotionally abused?

If you are being emotionally abused, like Nina, you probably feel that something is wrong with you. If you don't believe you are loved, then it will make you feel hurt, sad, and angry inside. You probably are having trouble making friends and may lash out toward others in hurtful ways. It is also difficult to concentrate on schoolwork if you can't sleep well at night, are hungry, or are worried about family members being hurt while you are away from the house.

### Why do my parents hurt me this way?

Often, parents don't realize how hurtful their actions are. They probably just treat you the same way they were treated by their parents. In fact, some experts say that parents are six times more likely to abuse their own children if they were abused themselves. Your parents may not have realistic expectations for you. Or maybe they find the responsibility of being parents overwhelming.

### How can I recognize emotional abuse?

Although emotional abuse can be difficult to identify, your behavior will give clues about how you feel about yourself. If you don't feel good about yourself because you have been abused, you might be lashing out at others. Do you steal, fight, lie, bully younger children, or hurt animals? Do you withdraw by not sharing any of your feelings with others? These actions could indicate that something is wrong at home.

### Can emotional abuse lead to physical abuse?

Yes, it can. That's one more reason why it's important to

get help for the whole family when emotional abuse is recognized.

### Signs of Emotional Abuse

Unless the abuse is very severe, it can be difficult to identify. Here are some questions you can ask yourself. On a piece of paper, write the numbers 1 through 6 in a column. For each question, write one of the following responses that best answers the question for you:

*Never*

*Most of the time*

*Always*

If you write "Never" for more than two questions, you may need to talk with someone about your relationship with your parents. If you answer "Most of the Time" or "Always" to most of these questions, give your parents a hug and thank them for being there for you.

1. Do you feel that your parents care about your overall well-being?

2. Do they make you feel like you are important to them?

3. If they leave you alone, do they tell you where they are going and how you can reach them?

4. Are you provided with adequate food, shelter, and clothing?

5. Are you allowed to have friends your own age?

6. Are you sometimes allowed to have friends visit you at home?

If other things are happening in your home that bother you, even if they are not listed above, it is important to share your feelings with your family. Here are some things you can do.

1. Make a list of the things that bother you.

2. Tell your parents you want to talk to them about some things that have been bothering you.

3. Pick a quiet time to talk with family members. For example, don't try to do this in the morning when everyone is trying to get ready for work or school, or as soon as people get home in the evening.

Some parents will try hard to listen and some won't. If talking with them doesn't work for you, and your parents remain emotionally abusive, you will feel hurt, sad, and angry, but don't give up trying to get help. Reach out to other adults whom you feel comfortable talking with.

## CHAPTER THREE

# *Sibling Abuse*

"Please don't leave, Mommy. Please stay with me. I don't want you to leave," Tyler sobbed.

"Stop it, Tyler, you're acting like a two-year-old. What's wrong with you? You're almost eight years old, and Tom is twelve. I should be able to leave you two alone for a couple of hours while I go out shopping. Now go in your room and play."

Tyler watched his mother walk out the door. He heard the car back out of the driveway. Heading down the hall toward his bedroom, Tyler wondered where his older brother was hiding. His stomach tightened as he tried to get ready for a door to fly open and Tom to jump out. It was definitely too quiet in the house. Tyler had just made it to his bedroom door when he suddenly tripped and fell, landing flat on his face. Before he could catch his breath, Tom was on top of him, pinning Tyler's hands to his side.

"Get off me, Tom! I'm going to tell Mom."

"What a crybaby you are. 'I'm telling Mom, I'm telling Mom,'" Tom mimicked, slapping Tyler on the head.

"Get off me—I mean it," Tyler yelled, moving his body from side to side, trying to hold back the tears that were welling up. "I hate you!"

Tom held Tyler's arms tighter and leaned over him. "Wimp, if you open your mouth, I'll set you on fire some night when you're sleeping. So shut up!"

Tom finally got up, leaving his brother on the floor. Tyler saw a broom lying across the floor and realized that that was how Tom had tripped him. Tyler waited until he heard the TV come on, then he got up, ran into his room, and flopped across his bed. He hated his brother and wished he would die, and he hated his mother for not protecting him from Tom.

### Isn't fighting between siblings normal?

Disagreements and fights are a normal part of growing up with a brother or sister. Feeling jealous or resentful from time to time is also common. Boys tend to fight physically with each other and girls fight more with words. Most disagreements between brothers and sisters can be worked out without anyone getting hurt.

### When does it become abusive?

Fighting between brothers and sisters becomes abusive if one sibling has some kind of power over another. The brother or sister who is abused is usually weaker or younger or feels unable to stop the abuse. The abusive sibling uses threats to make the other afraid to tell, as when Tom said to Tyler, "I'll set you on fire." The physical abuse might include hitting, punching, tying up, or sexual touching.

### Why didn't Tyler's mother protect him from his brother?

She probably thought Tyler was just acting up to keep her from going out. Many parents don't realize the extent of the abuse that is going on, and they don't understand just how afraid the younger sibling is. Other times, parents feel that kids can work out their disagreements themselves.

### What about sexual contact between siblings?

Sexual contact—including touching the penis or vulva with the hands, tongue, or mouth, inserting a finger or object into the vagina or anus, and intercourse—can occur between two brothers, two sisters, a brother and a sister, or stepbrothers and stepsisters.

Young children are very curious about sex, and some looking, exploring, and touching is normal. Sometimes this is done by playing "doctor." However, it is not acceptable to threaten or force someone to touch or be touched. What may start out as curiosity can turn into forced sexual contact—in other words, rape.

### Can tickling be abusive?

If certain limits are respected, tickling can be harmless. The rule is simple. When the person being tickled says "Stop," the person doing the tickling *stops immediately.*

Sometimes, however, tickling is used as a way to gain power over a person. For example, if you tickle your brother until he wets his pants or starts to cry, that is humiliating for him. Also, tickling can be used as a way to touch some-one's body in inappropriate places, such as the penis, breasts, vulva, or buttocks. What starts out as a fun game can turn into a painful experience. You may feel uncomfortable be-cause you have been touched in a sexual way, but you might excuse the behavior, thinking it was done by accident.

If tickling becomes confusing or painful for you, be very firm and say loudly, "Stop! You are hurting me." Sometimes that is all it takes to stop the game. Tell the person who tickled you that you were uncomfortable and that you don't want to play the game again. If he or she doesn't listen to you, tell a trusted adult.

**Why do I hit my younger brothers and sisters?**

There are probably many reasons why you do it. Some of these reasons could be anger, boredom, jealousy, or the feeling that your parent is giving you too much responsi-bility and not enough freedom to do the things you want to do. It is all right to have these feelings, but it is not all right to hurt other people.

**My brothers and sisters and I fight all the time.**
**Will we ever like each other?**

Most brothers and sisters become friends as they grow up. The friendship happens over time, as each of you develops your own interests and becomes more sure of your own special place within the family. If, however, there has been physical, emotional, or sexual abuse among you and your siblings, then you will probably need to come to terms with your hurt and angry feelings before you can have a meaningful relationship. Sometimes we never get past these feelings, and it is impossible to have a healthy, close relationship with a sibling. Sometimes, too, siblings just grow apart and don't spend time with each other as adults.

### How can I get along better with my brothers and sisters?

Remember, most squabbles and disagreements are a normal part of growing up and living in a family. Disagreements teach us how to speak up for ourselves, understand others' views, and compromise. Compromise, without the use of force, is an important skill to learn when you are young. Try talking with your brother or sister and see if you can set some rules together. Write down the solutions you come up with on a piece of paper, then both of you sign it, so you have something to refer to if you have another fight.

### Signs of Sibling Abuse

- Has one of your brothers or sisters ever played with or threatened you with a weapon such as a knife or gun?
- Do you hear threats such as, "If you tell I'll kill you," or "I'll tell everyone at school that you're a slut"?
- Do you abuse animals by tying them up, setting them on fire, or stabbing them, or have you seen a brother or sister hurt animals?
- Do your siblings play with matches or set fires?
- Have you been sexually abused by your brother or sister?

If any of these things are happening in your home, you need to seek the help of an adult who will listen to you.

# Chapter Four

# *Incest*

Tucking the covers tightly around her neck and along her sides, Janie sighed deeply and lay still on her bed. She stared at the sliver of light shining through the crack between her bedroom door and the floor. Focusing on the unbroken light relaxed her enough so that her thumping heart didn't seem to vibrate in her head so much. Even though it was past eleven, she had to try to stay awake. Waiting—listening—hoping.

"What's the use of hoping, Janie?" she asked herself. "You know he will come and you know what he will do."

A chill came over her and her body shook. She felt tears welling up. Feeling frozen, she drifted to sleep.

"Janie, are you awake? It's your daddy."

At first Janie thought she was dreaming, but then she felt the familiar hand rubbing her breast. Even through her heavy sweatshirt and bra, she knew the feel of his large, rough hands rubbing and squeezing her. He tried to move his other hand under the covers. Janie lay deathly still. He fumbled impatiently with the blankets until they pulled away from her, leaving just enough room on the bed for him to slide his body next to hers.

Janie remained still, refocusing her eyes to the ceiling and separating her mind from what was happening to her body. It was like she was watching a movie of someone else, from above. She heard the words he always whispered.

"You are my special girl. I love you, Janie. Your mother doesn't understand me. I need more love than she can give me—and I love you better, anyway."

Janie wondered where her mother was and why she didn't hear him. Why hadn't her mother stopped him over the last three years? Where has she been since I was nine years old, Janie thought, fighting back nausea as she felt her father push her hand down around his erect penis. Her breath was taken away by the weight of him on top of her, and she squeezed her eyes shut.

### What is incest?

Incest is sexual contact between members of the same family. Sexual contact includes touching or rubbing of genitals, any contact between the mouth or tongue and genitals, and intercourse, which is penetration, however slight, of the vagina or anus by a penis or object. Being forced to look at sexual pictures or movies, having to watch someone masturbate, or being forced to help someone else masturbate are also forms of sexual abuse.

It is estimated that one in three girls and one in six boys experience some form of sexual abuse.

### Who are the abusers?

Any family member can be an abuser: fathers, grandfathers, brothers, sisters, uncles, aunts, mothers, grandmothers, stepparents, or a parent's girlfriend or boyfriend.

### Are the victims always female?

No! Many of the victims are males. Boys suffer the same feelings of confusion, anger, hurt, and fear as girls.

### Aren't boys abused just by gay men?

No. Most of the males who sexually assault other males are heterosexual. Sexual abuse is usually an act of power and control, not sexual passion.

### If I'm being sexually abused and I get an erection, does that mean I wanted it to happen?

Sometimes males are forced into a state of arousal by the abuser. The erection is simply a physical response, and it does not mean you wanted to be hurt, violated, or humiliated.

### Why does Janie's father abuse her?

Janie's father turns to her to meet his own needs. He has low self-esteem and acts aggressively toward his daughter by having sex with her to make himself feel more powerful. He probably feels inadequate in his relationship with Janie's mother and turns to Janie to feel he has power and control.

### Janie's dad says he loves her—doesn't that make a difference?

Janie's dad does not show his love in a healthy way. Healthy love is never secret and never forced on someone. He has broken the basic bond of trust between himself and his child. He abuses Janie by using her to fulfill his own adult needs.

### Why doesn't Janie stop him?

Janie probably has tried to stop him at one time, but she feels a sense of loyalty to her father and her family. She feels confused and helpless. Adults who abuse children have many ways to make them keep the secret. The abuser may threaten to harm the child, another family member, or a pet. "If you don't let me do it to you, I'll do it to your younger sister" is a common and powerful threat. The adult may tell the child that no one will believe her or that she will be blamed for allowing it to happen. Janie may be afraid her father will never love her again or that he will hurt her. She might be afraid that if she tells her mother, she will collapse in grief or kick Janie out of the house in anger.

### What are the effects of incest?

Sexual abuse leads to intense feelings of shame. The victim may feel dirty, ugly, or worthless. If you are or have been a victim of incest, you will probably have difficulty trusting other people and dealing with your sexuality. You likely will feel anger over the loss of your childhood, safety, and self-esteem, as well as a great sense of guilt, especially if any part of the incest felt good. You may feel that you are different and spend much of your time alone. Maybe you cannot even admit to yourself that the incest happened. Sometimes victims totally block out, or can't remember, the incest. These are all normal feelings and reactions. It is important to talk about your feelings with a professional counselor who understands the effects of incest.

### Why doesn't Janie's mother stop the abuse?

Maybe Janie's mother doesn't know that her daughter is being abused. Perhaps she is being hurt physically by her husband, and she feels unable to stop him from abusing Janie. Some mothers feel pressure to have a "perfect family" or a family that is respected in the community. In other cases, the mother may have been sexually abused as a child herself. She may not know how to deal with the abuse of her child, or she could be afraid to face the issue.

Some mothers want to leave their abusive husbands, but they think they don't have the skills to earn enough money to support themselves and their children. Other mothers may blame the child instead of the husband for the abuse, even though it is not the child's fault.

Unless the mother is also involved in the incest, she should not be blamed for her husband's actions. However, once she becomes aware of any abuse, she should take action.

### Are there other kinds of sexual assault?

Some kinds of sexual assault involve no physical contact. A child might be forced to look at another person's genitals, to watch sexual movies, or to look at sexual pictures. Sometimes sexual abuse is subtle, such as when a mother walks around with bare breasts or a father sits around the house with nothing on. Being encouraged to watch adults have sexual intercourse is also abusive.

### Is it common for young people to separate their minds from their bodies during an assault?

The emotional and sometimes physical pain of sexual

abuse is so great that the victim has to find a way to deal with it. Many incest survivors report that they mentally left their bodies during the abuse and felt like they were watching from above or from a corner of the room.

### Is the abuse Janie's fault?

No, Janie is not to blame for what her father is doing. It is always the adult's fault for touching or saying things that make a young person feel scared or hurt.

### What can Janie do?

Janie or anyone who is being sexually abused needs to find an adult who will help. If you tell someone in your family and that person doesn't help you, tell a teacher whom you trust or another adult, such as a religious leader, school counselor, your best friend's parent, or a youth leader. Tell a librarian or look in the phone book under Child Protective Services or Rape Crisis Center. If the first person you tell doesn't believe you, tell someone else.

### Will Janie be sent away for telling?

By telling someone, Janie will get the protection she needs. Maybe she will have to go to another place to live for a while, but not because she is bad. Her father may have to go to counseling or leave the home and go to court or even to jail. If this happens, it is because of what he did, not because Janie caused it to happen. The separation could be a step toward saving the family.

### Signs of Incest

- Is someone in your family touching or rubbing you on

your breast, vulva, penis, or anus, or is someone making you touch him or her?

- Is a family member making you keep secrets by threatening you?
- Has a family member told you that the sexual contact is your fault and you will get in trouble if you tell anyone?
- Has someone in your family offered you money or other gifts in exchange for looking at or taking pictures of your nude body?
- Has someone in your family said to you that he or she is "teaching you about love" while forcing you to have sexual contact?

If you answer yes to any of these questions, get help right away. Talk with an adult you trust about what is happening. Remember, it is not your fault and you have the *right* to tell someone in order to stop the abuse. If the abuser is also physically violent at times, be sure to explain that as well, so that special care can be taken for your protection.

# CHAPTER FIVE

# *Elder Abuse*

Sara felt sad as she watched her grandma sitting at the table staring at the dish of food in front of her. Sara tried to help her, hoping her mother wouldn't turn from the stove and catch her spoon-feeding Grandma.

Sara had wonderful memories of happier times when her dad was alive and they would all visit Grandma and Grandpa Stone for a week during the summer.

"Remember the pot roast you used to make for us, Grandma?" Sara asked, forgetting about her mother.

"Yes, Sara. And I also remember you and Grandpa Bill licking the gravy pan and fighting over who would get the crispy pieces."

Sara's laugh was interrupted by her mother's sharp tone.

"Funny you can remember way back then, Ma, but you can't remember to pick up your clothes or wash your face and brush your teeth."

Grandma Stone lowered her eyes and started to make clicking noises with her tongue.

Sara touched her grandmother's shoulder, hoping to catch her attention again. She wanted her to stop making that sound.

"That noise drives me crazy," Sara's mother said. "She does it on purpose just to get me upset."

Sara did not believe this—not the part about her grandmother doing it on purpose, anyway. But there was no way to convince her mother. They had had many arguments about Grandma and Sara didn't want to get into another one tonight.

Sara tried to understand her mother's feelings. But it was hard sometimes, especially when she knew that her mother was taking out her anger on Grandma. Ever since Dad had died two years ago, it seemed like her mother had gotten more and more resentful toward her mother—Grandma. Sara had often heard her mother yelling at Grandma, and recently she saw some bruises on her arms. She decided to help her mother more with Grandma's care.

"Maybe that will help," she thought, picking up the spoon to help her grandmother with one more bite.

## What is elder abuse?

Elder abuse is the mistreatment of an older family member by a younger one. It can include not taking physical care of the person, yelling or swearing at the person, giving the person too much medicine, taking the person's money away, or pinching, hitting, kicking, or slapping the older person.

Elder abuse sometimes happens in nursing homes and

other care facilities, where workers might give older people too much medicine or physically restrain them.

### Why would Sara's mother mistreat her mother?

Sometimes when people grow older they become sick and need a lot of care. Sara's mother may feel angry that she has to take care of another person, especially without the help of her husband. Maybe it is inconvenient for the grand-mother to live with Sara's mother, but she would feel guilty about placing her in a nursing home. Or she might feel that she can't do what she wants because caring for the grand-mother takes up so much time. These kinds of frustrations may lead to abuse. For example, if Grandma doesn't eat her meals fast enough, Sara's mother might slap her.

### What makes elderly people forget things?

Forgetfulness is part of the aging process. Sometimes el-derly people can remember things that happened many years ago, but they forget their name or address. They don't do this on purpose; it only means that part of the brain isn't functioning the way it used to.

### Why don't I ever hear about elder abuse?

Most elder abuse is not reported to anyone. The elderly often depend on their abusers for food, shelter, and cloth-ing. They may feel confused, ashamed, or embarrassed to admit that someone they love is mistreating them. Some-times they just do not know whom to tell.

### What can Sara do to help?

Sara and her mother could talk about what kinds of care

the grandmother needs, and they could share the tasks. Making a schedule will lift some of the burden from Sara's mother. If other family members live nearby, they should be asked to share the responsibility also. Many communities have programs and services for the elderly. Find out what services are available in your community. Setting up a support system ensures that the burden doesn't fall on just one person, and there is less resentment toward the elderly relative.

### Signs of Elder Abuse

- Do you see physical signs of abuse, such as cuts, rope burns, bruises, black eyes, or bleeding? Is the elderly person heavily sedated with medication?
- Does the person have dirty clothes, body odor, matted hair, no teeth, or improper eyeglasses?
- Does the older person ask you for money?

If you answer yes to any of these questions, it is possible that your elderly relative is being abused. Call your local Department of Human Services or the police.

# CHAPTER SIX

# *Domestic Abuse*

"Name?"

"Sheila."

"Address?"

"Fifteen-twenty-four Willow Drive."

"Home phone?"

"It was disconnected."

"Any children?"

"Four."

Sheila shifted the baby to the other side of her lap. Her arm was bruised and throbbing, and her mouth was dry, as if someone had stuffed cotton in it. Her lips were split and swollen. It was hard for her to focus on the woman asking questions from the other side of the desk, because Sheila's glasses had been broken earlier when she was knocked against a wall. Although her head was pounding, Sheila's main concern was for her three children waiting in the next room.

"What did you say?" Sheila asked, realizing that she wasn't paying attention.

"Would you like me to stop for a while? Can I get you some water or hold the baby for you?"

Sheila clutched the baby closer and shook her head.

The woman leaned over the desk and put her hand on Sheila's shoulder. "I'm sorry this has happened. You are safe here. My name is Nancy."

"Oh, Nancy, could I see my other children just for a minute, before I finish answering the questions?"

"No problem, they're in the playroom next door."

Sheila handed the sleeping baby to Nancy and started to get up. She hadn't realized how badly shaken she was. It seemed like she could hardly walk.

"Why don't you stay here and I'll have the children come in," Nancy said.

Sheila was relieved. She put her elbow on the table and rested. Images of the evening flashed in her mind, and she could hear the sound of screaming in her ears. When her husband had come home from work and found her lying down instead of fixing dinner, he didn't ask if she was sick. He just started yelling about how she was a lazy wife.

Nancy stopped when she got to the door leading into the shelter's playroom. She saw Sheila's children huddled in a corner talking with the child advocate. Nancy decided to wait a few minutes before going in, to allow the advocate to calm the children down.

"I'm not scared of being hit, I'm tough," Bobby, the oldest of the three, was saying.

"I'm no sissy like her," he continued, pointing to his younger sister, who was sobbing.

"Shut up now. You'll wake her up," he said, poking his sister on the arm and pointing to the third child, who was curled up in a ball on the floor, sucking her thumb.

"Bobby, when boys your age come to the shelter, even bigger boys than you, they feel scared. Sometimes they feel so scared they wet their pants or cry," the advocate said.

"Nah, only sissies cry or pee their pants. I've been here before. Still got that big red wagon you had before?" Bobby asked.

"Bobby, what is your sister's name?"

"That's Gina. Gina, shut up!"

"Bobby, I think Gina is scared. Let's see if she will sit with me. Gina, do you want to sit on my lap?"

Gina crawled into her lap, keeping her head tucked in her collar.

"Bobby, what do you think Gina is thinking?"

"She thinks she did something bad and that's why we had to come here."

"That's right, Bobby, what else?"

"That Mama will be dead and we will be sent away.

"She doesn't want to go to a new school and she doesn't like all these big people around here," Bobby continued.

The baby was stirring in Nancy's arms, so she went into the playroom. Bobby looked startled as Nancy walked toward them. His face had started to relax a little while he was talking, but now it tensed up again and he looked defiant.

"That's our baby, where's my mama?"

"Yes, this is your sister. I'm just holding her for your mother. She is in the other room and wants to see you. Do you want to come with me to see her?"

Gina was up on her feet before Nancy had finished the

sentence. Bobby stayed close to Nancy's side, keeping an eye on the baby. Nancy walked them back to the room while the advocate picked up the other child from the floor.

"Can we go home now, Mama?"

"Are you okay? Can we go home?"

"Is Daddy going to jail?"

Hearing the nervous voices of her children, Sheila sat up and put her arms out to hug them. She didn't have all the answers for them, but one thing she knew for certain. For now, they were safe.

### What is domestic violence?

Domestic violence, spouse abuse, partner abuse, battering, and wife abuse are names used when a man or woman is mistreated by the adult partner he or she lives with. The children in the family are also affected by seeing the abuse or by being physically abused themselves.

Domestic violence also includes emotional, verbal, financial, and sexual abuse. Most often, if there is physical abuse, other kinds of abuse are also taking place.

### Are men ever abused?

Yes. Men are sometimes physically abused, but more often they are emotionally abused. Men are less likely to seek help, because they are afraid that no one will believe them or that they will be made fun of for not being "man" enough to control the woman.

### My father beats my mother.
### Why does she stay with him?

Some women depend on their husband or boyfriend for

food, shelter, and clothing for themselves and their children. They may not have the confidence in themselves necessary to survive on their own. They believe it when their partner says, "You'll never make it without me." A woman might be afraid to leave because her husband has threatened to find her and kill her. Some women stay because of cultural or religious reasons. Other reasons may include a feeling of shame about the abuse, a belief that she deserves the abuse, or a hope that somehow the abuser will change and the abuse will end.

**Why does my father beat my mother?**

Your father probably feels angry inside and lashes out physically to release his feelings. His anger may have nothing do to with anything your mother did, but hitting her is a way for him to feel he has power and control over his surroundings. This does not make abusive behavior okay, however.

**What can I do to protect my mother?**

As much as it hurts you to see your mother being hit, once the abuse has started, it is best to get yourself and any other children to a safe place. Some kids who have tried to help their mothers end up getting hurt themselves. *Don't try to stop the abuse yourself.* Call the police, go to a neighbor, or tell your teacher or any other adult who can help you.

**I am always worrying about my family—
what can I do?**

Living in a violent home is very stressful and frightening.

You may have serious concerns: will it happen again? Is my mother hurt? Is she dead? Will my family split up? Will my father go to jail? When you see and hear fighting between the adults in your family, it can be difficult to concentrate on other things or go to sleep. Maybe you feel guilty for wishing that your parents were dead or feel that somehow you caused the abuse. Remember, you are never responsible for the behavior of the adults in your family.

### What does a shelter look like?

Many shelters for battered women and their children are set up like a home, with a living room, dining room, kitchen, bedrooms, and a play area. Everyone shares in the work of setting the table, sweeping the floors, doing the dishes, dusting, making the beds, and picking up toys.

### Wouldn't I feel sad if I had to go to a shelter?

You probably would feel sad. You also might feel mad at the person who did the abuse, mad at your mother for not stopping the abuse, and scared because you don't know what will happen to you. You will miss your friends, pets, toys, and even your school. All these feelings are normal. In some shelters, workers called child advocates will talk with you about your feelings. Along with the bad feelings, you may also feel safe—and relieved that the abuse has stopped.

### Am I to blame for the fighting?

You did not cause the fighting between your parents. It didn't happen because you didn't clean your room or forgot to take out the garbage. And it wasn't because you aren't doing well in school. The abuse was caused by the adult and the way he or she has chosen to deal with problems and conflicts.

### What will happen to my family if my father is arrested?

If your father is arrested, he will be handcuffed with his arms behind him and taken to the police station. There, the police will take his picture and fingerprints and ask him questions. He will be placed in jail and must stay there until he goes before a judge in the courtroom. The judge will decide what punishment he should receive and will determine whether the family needs help. Social service agencies can sometimes give the family money for food, rent, and utilities. Some abusers have to go to jail. Other times the judge may order the person to get counseling. Unfortunately, an arrest doesn't always stop the abuser from going back and starting the abuse again.

It's scary to see someone you love taken away in handcuffs. You may blame yourself or the person who called the police. You probably want the abuse to stop, but you don't want your parent to get into trouble. Family violence doesn't usually stop on its own, though. For that reason, it is important to report the abuse, before it gets worse.

### The Cycle of Violence

Domestic violence usually follows a predictable pattern, which is often referred to as "the cycle of violence." The cycle of violence usually has three stages:

1. During the first stage, tension builds in the abuser. There may be minor arguments and some pushing or slapping. The victim tries to please or humor the abuser.

2. The tension builds until there is a conflict that leads to a full attack—this is the second stage. Once the violence starts, there is usually nothing the victim can do to stop it.

3. After the violence occurs, the abusive person feels ashamed and guilty and may promise never to do it again. He or she may cry, plead forgiveness, and give presents to the victim.

In time, the third stage passes, the tension starts to build again, and the cycle continues.

## Cycle of Violence

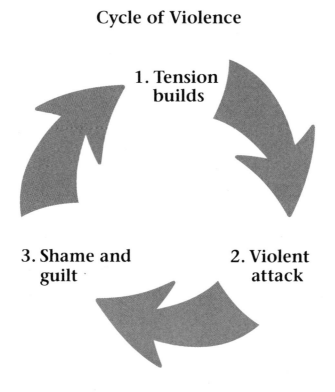

**1. Tension builds**

**2. Violent attack**

**3. Shame and guilt**

### Signs of Domestic Abuse

- Does your mother wear dark glasses to cover up a black eye?
- Have you seen your parents slapping, pushing, or hitting each other?
- Does your mother explain her bruises or injuries by saying she fell or is clumsy?
- Does your mother spend a lot of time alone crying?
- Is there more fighting in your home when one of your parents is drinking?

Domestic abuse is a crime that can result in serious injury and even death. It usually gets worse as time goes on, and the risk of serious injury increases. If domestic abuse is going on in your family, let someone you trust know as soon as possible.

# CHAPTER SEVEN

# *Self-Esteem*

Self-esteem is a word used to describe how and what we think and feel about ourselves. These thoughts and feelings stem from the experiences and relationships that we have from the time we are babies to the present. Our early relationships with our parents and other family members play a major role in whether we have a positive or negative self-image.

Positive experiences help build our self-esteem. For example, if you were told that you were a beautiful, worthwhile person, that you would be loved even if you made mistakes, and that you had talents and abilities, you would probably develop high self-esteem. If, on the other hand, you were told that you were stupid, lazy, or ugly, or if the people close to you abused you physically, emotionally, or sexually, then you would probably think you were not worthy of love or that you couldn't do anything right. Your self-esteem would likely be low—it would be hard to like yourself or to have confidence in yourself. But no one person or event can determine your level of self-esteem. Self-esteem develops over time as we change and have different experiences, such as friendships with classmates and teachers, and success or difficulty with schoolwork, sports, or hobbies.

Feeling good about who you are is important to your overall health and well-being. If you like and respect yourself and believe you are a good person, then you will expect to be treated well by others. If, on the other hand, you don't like yourself and feel that you don't deserve respect, then you may treat yourself badly or allow others to treat you badly. For example, you might start using drugs or alcohol, run away from home, or have trouble making friends.

People with high self-esteem are happy about who they are and what they can accomplish. They are able to develop close relationships with others. High self-esteem helps you achieve your goals, enjoy other people's company, and accept new ideas, experiences, and changes. If you have low self-esteem, you probably feel isolated and alone. You might be afraid to try new things because you believe that you will fail. You feel you have no control over what happens in your life.

Having high self-esteem doesn't mean that you won't feel bad about yourself from time to time, or disappointed in the way others treat you. Self-esteem is not the same as self-centeredness or arrogance. Generally, self-centered people are covering their feelings of low self-esteem. They put down other people's talents and accomplishments in order to make themselves feel better. People with high self-esteem are glad about others' accomplishments as well as their own.

Do you have high self-esteem or low self-esteem? To find out, take two pieces of paper. At the top of one piece of paper, write, "The Things I Like about Myself." On the second piece, write, "The Things I Dislike about Myself." Before you begin, remember that everybody feels bad about themselves from time to time. When you make your lists, think about how you feel *most* of the time.

List all your good qualities and the things you admire about yourself, such as your gentleness with animals, your artistic ability, your skills in football or biking, your nice smile, beautiful hair, or straight teeth. List even the little things.

Next, list the things you don't like about yourself on the second sheet. When you've finished, compare both lists. Which is longer? If you have been able to list more things you like about yourself than those you dislike, you probably feel good about yourself and are developing high self-esteem.

If you have listed more things you dislike about yourself than things you like, then you probably are having difficulty with your self-esteem. Regardless of what your list says, there are many things you can do to improve your self-esteem:

1. *Acceptance.* Accept that you have good qualities and that weaknesses can become strengths. Work on changing the things that you don't like, but if there's something about yourself that you don't like and cannot change, learn to accept it. For example, maybe you don't like your big feet, but since you can't make them smaller, learn to accept them.

2. *Praise.* Give yourself praise for the things you have done that you like. Look at the list of the things that you like about yourself. Take pride in them.

3. *Time.* Learn to enjoy your own company. Allow yourself to daydream. Instead of feeling sad that you don't have someone to do something with, enjoy reading a book, taking a walk, or working on a craft project.

4. *Encouragement.* Encourage yourself by doing self-talk. When a negative thought comes into your mind, such as, "I'm stupid, look at this terrible grade I got on my paper," replace it by saying, "I will learn from the mistakes I made and do better next time."

5. *Be realistic.* Set goals that are realistic for you to achieve. An unrealistic goal will reinforce your feelings of not being smart enough or good enough. For example, if you would like to lose 30 pounds, it would be unrealistic to expect to do that in one month.

6. *Respect your body.* Don't hurt your body by smoking or taking drugs or alcohol. Eat lots of vegetables and fruits instead of candy. Exercise.

7. *Trust.* Act on what you think and feel is right, regardless of what others are doing. Listen to that little voice inside you and start trusting it.

8. *Love yourself.* Don't overreact about the mistakes you make. Accept and learn from them. Remind yourself that you are a good person.

Living in a violent home can damage your self-esteem. Recovering from this kind of abuse takes time. It involves relearning things you have seen and been told. Just by reading this book, you have taken the first step toward recovery —learning the facts and where to go for help.

You *can* improve your self-esteem, and if you need outside help, there are people in your community who can help you—all you have to do is reach out. Several social service agencies are listed in the back of this book. You may feel scared or shy about seeking help—this is normal. Recovery is a slow process and won't happen overnight. Just remember to keep calling until you find someone who listens and helps you.

# CONCLUSION

Family violence teaches you that the way to deal with conflict is to lash out physically or verbally. It teaches you to try to make yourself feel better by taking power and control away from others. These attitudes, learned in childhood, are passed down from one generation to the next. They must be changed. Family violence is not a private matter, because it affects each of us—the whole society.

If you live in a violent home, you may be experiencing depression, fear, anxiety, sadness, difficulty sleeping, guilt, or problems with eating. You probably live in constant fear of being injured. You may feel guilty about loving or hating the abuser. You might hate one of your parents for not stopping the abuse or for not believing that it is happening. You may feel helpless because you can't stop the violence yourself.

I know how awful those feelings are, because I grew up in

an abusive home and I couldn't concentrate on my schoolwork or enjoy other activities. My feelings of fear, anger, and sadness also caused me to make poor decisions and to hurt myself, because I thought I deserved it. But I didn't deserve to be abused, and neither do you or any human being.

Just in the time it has taken me to write the last two pages of this book, three tragic incidents have occurred in my community as a result of family violence. The first story is about an 11-year-old boy who killed himself because "he couldn't take it anymore." The "it" was being beaten by his stepfather. The boy stopped the violence by ending his life.

The second story is about a 17-year-old girl who shot her father in the head. When asked why she did it, she said, "To stop the hurt." The "hurt" was incest.

The final story is about a 13-year-old boy who ran away from home because he was sexually abused by his mother's boyfriend. The boy was picked up at a bus station by an older man who offered to let him live with him in exchange for sex. The boy contracted AIDS.

In every community throughout the country, there are stories like these, which happen as a result of some form of family violence. The most tragic part of these stories is that the young people didn't know that there were other ways to stop the abuse.

Family violence is a crime and it is against the law. It is very important that you understand that you are not to blame for the actions of adults, regardless of what they tell you. You didn't do anything to deserve the abuse and you have the right to find someone to help you stop it. You can help stop the cycle of abuse instead of letting violence become a part of your life.

Family violence is a crime committed in secrecy, in the home, against someone who the abuser feels will always keep the secret. That is the abuser's power. You can take that power away from him or her by telling someone.

# *Resources*

You can write to these national organizations for free information:

American Association for the Protection of Children,
Division of the American Humane Association
63 Inverness Drive E.
Englewood, CO 80112

Childhelp USA
P.O. Box 4175
Woodland Hills, CA 91370

Clearinghouse on Child Abuse and Neglect Information
P.O. Box 1182
Washington, DC 20013

National Aging Resource Center on Elder Abuse (NARCEA)
810 1st Street NE, Suite 500
Washington, DC 20002

National Coalition Against Domestic Violence
P.O. Box 34103
Washington, DC 20043-4103

National Committee for the Prevention of Child Abuse
332 S. Michigan Avenue, Suite 1600
Chicago, IL 60604

National Committee for the Prevention of Elder Abuse
c/o The Institute on Aging
The Medical Center of Central Massachusetts
119 Belmont Street
Worcester, MA 01605

Parents Anonymous National Office
6733 S. Sepulveda Blvd., Suite 270
Los Angeles, CA 90045

## Hotline Numbers

Adolescent Suicide Hotline
1-800-621-4000

Al-Anon and Alateen
1-800-356-9996

Alzheimer's Information and Referral Service
1-800-621-0379

Childhelp USA
1-800-422-4453

Family Service America
1-800-221-2681

National Council on Child Abuse and Family Violence
1-800-222-2000

National Domestic Violence Hotline
1-800-333-7233

National Runaway Switchboard
1-800-621-4000

Parents Anonymous
1-800-421-0353

You can look for local resources in your telephone book under these headings:

Child Abuse Hotline
Children's Protective Services
Hospital Emergency Rooms
Mental Health Centers
Police (or call 911 or 0 for operator)
Public Health Authorities
School Nurse or Counseling Department
Social Service Agencies
Welfare Department

# *For Further Reading*

Gilbert, Sara. *Get Help: Solving the Problems in Your Life.*
New York: Morrow Junior Books, 1989.

Kurland, Morton L. *Coping with Family Violence.* Rev. ed.
New York: The Rosen Publishing Group, 1990.

O'Brien, Shirley. *Child Abuse, A Crying Shame.* Salt Lake City:
Brigham Young University Press, 1980.

Rosenberg, Ellen. *Growing Up Feeling Good: A Growing Up
Handbook Especially for Kids.* New York: Penguin Books, 1989.

Taylor, Paul M., and Diane B. Taylor. *Coping with a Dysfunctional
Family.* New York: The Rosen Publishing Group, 1990.

Zerafa, Judy. *Go For It.* Workman Publishing, 1982.

# INDEX

## Other helpful books from Lerner's Coping with Modern Issues series:

**Celebrate You!**
Building Your Self-Esteem
*by Julie Tallard Johnson*

**Coping with Death and Grief**
*by Marge Eaton Heegaard*

**Eating Disorders**
A Question and Answer Book
about Anorexia Nervosa and
Bulimia Nervosa
*by Ellen Erlanger*

**Feeling Safe, Feeling Strong**
How to Avoid Sexual Abuse
and What to Do If It Happens
to You
*by Susan Neiburg Terkel and
Janice E. Rench*

**Teen Pregnancy**
*by Sonia Bowe-Gutman*

**Teen Sexuality**
Decisions and Choices
*by Janice E. Rench*

**Teen Suicide**
A Book for Friends,
Family, and Classmates
*by Janet Kolehmainen and
Sandra Handwerk*

**Understanding AIDS**
*by Ethan A. Lerner, M.D., Ph.D.*

**SPANISH EDITION:**
Comprendiendo el SIDA
*by Ethan A. Lerner, M.D., Ph.D.*

**Understanding Mental Illness**
For Teens Who Care about
Someone with Mental Illness
*by Julie Tallard Johnson*

**Understanding Sexual Identity**
For Gay and Lesbian Teens
and Their Friends
*by Janice E. Rench*